AF345542

Mind Games

John Tischer

Copyright© 2021 John Tischer
ISBN: 978-93-88319-57-7

First Edition: 2021
Rs. 200/-

Cyberwit.net
HIG 45 Kaushambi Kunj, Kalindipuram
Allahabad - 211011 (U.P.) India
http://www.cyberwit.net
Tel: +(91) 9415091004
E-mail: info@cyberwit.net

No part of this book may be reproduced or transmitted in any form or by
any means, electronic, mechanical, photocopying, or otherwise, without
the express written consent of John Tischer.

Printed at Thomson Press India Limited.

To my father, Irvin George Fredrivk Elizabeth Tischer

and to my teacher, Her Eminence Khandro Rinpoche

Contents

This is Now the Time

The monkeys don't even know they're caged,
in fact, they love the saccharine taste
of the bars as they lick them.

These marvelous flavors accumulated
over the decades of use: sweat, grease, vomit,
vaseline, blood and come mingle and swarm
as the hidden herbs of the universe,
swelling and rising over ecstatic buds of taste.

"We're done, my friend."
the leader of our group said
as he got up to go out,
into the limousine to his coke,
to his driver, to his so called life.

"It's all good, 84th and Lexington,
Save the Robot, they've got after hours till 6.
Grace Jones cut a guy's arm off last week.
Luckily he can still masturbate
as an arm challenged, disabled, urine stained
zipper individual.
It'll be live till dawn."

Reeking of brilliance,
My whisky soaked breath scares you
because you don't know what
you're going to get.

Yet, we all love it because
We breathe the same air, flesh
Rotten crotch,
manic laughter and
obsession with sex, ultimate
stupidity.

He even likes eating bison
nipples ripped immediately
off the milk filled breasts
of lactating, smelly, hairy
snorting monsters…chewing madly.

He was satisfied, for now…

Signifying particles or pure
intensities screethed across
the rusted gutters of rationality.

Copper tendrils eviscerated the
monopoly of a few golden arches…
the jewels began to shine in their eyes.

Luminosity is seeing that cables
may support the bridge but the metal
itself is a disease…yet, we only need
placebos because we're hypochondriacs.

Drinking six month old chunky
bitter, sour milk….mixed with frothy rotten
orange juice….emitting bubbles that tickle
the nostrils…..a whole in one…..the next level
was a sound bitten deli sandwich,
but the pickle was delicious…

it's back to the senses…
back to the senses now…
now senses the to back.

The old toad sat at the table
with an AK 47 chomping his cigar,
a beautiful salamander sucking his
AC/DC, which was a rich,
 jade green color with yellow
pus oozing slowly out of
a dozen bloody eruptions….

Meanwhile his drink was empty, so,
he screamed for the waitress. She slithered over
on her shiny tentacles and said:

"If you want a drink, tell me a joke"

"It's all good."

The salamander laughed so hard
she bit his organ off.
He kept laughing, he couldn't stop,
it felt like he was reliving his circumcision

The black holding the broom
smiled knowingly.

Echoing throughout the halls
and rooms and closets…
radiating out from the confessional
where I stood, my white collar askew.

My night with the living dead was very
intimate. I found myself pre-dead,
already dead, dead with a minimal
chance of survival.

When I take off my collar and get undressed
and go to bed I don't know what
religion I dream.

Mel Gibson stumbled into the bar,
eyes bleary with Jesus: "You're it!
You were born to play Jesus! What's your name?!!"
"Toshiro Mifune….how's Katie Yates these days?
I'm really interested in your process with George,
if you don't mind my looking into your oven….
because I'm allergic to Japanese food."

The Purge Of Evil (2012)

For everything there is a season.
This is the time of hell on earth.
This is the time of the flowering of evil.
The Lords of Materialism have seized power…
It is their time.

The karma they accumulate from their evil deeds
Will rid the world of them for a long time….
They will not be reborn as human.
It is the time of the purge of evil.

Remain human!
Don't get sucked into their trip!
This has to happen now!
Remain human! Remain human!
Don't give into their bloody game!
What goes around comes around!
Cultivate compassion!
The leaders are lost in lust!
Their self-destruction is inevitable!

A Condemned Man Looks Out A Palace Window

Doppelgänger, simulacrum wish you were here
instead of me
grim luxury
fresh air
guillotine
half a hamburger in the fridge
anticipating a beautiful storm
lightning, thunder, the works
charming self harpoon of circumstance
domination of the arcs
the foreground is clear
background red, hazy, fear.

Air In The Morning

Wafting air breeze sun and clouds
chaotic atomic decadence dance
sharp amoebic disingenuousness
slap in the face thanks…needed that
words with meaning drip dry ready
on the rocks in the bag over the target
all I need is a windmill
straight up
no chaser.

American Moloch

The old gods wear the bodies
that wear the suits.
Baal sitting in the diner
doesn't leave a tip.
Loki in his Lamborghini,
Satan in his sedan.

The curtain is the clothes they wear,
the mansions they live in,
their ceramic smiles,
the lies laced with larceny.

A movable beast, on the go,
fragmented into shards of darkness,
shivering with delight
at the actions they perform…
a whitewash if ever there was one.

Embodiment of evil, what did it take
to sign on the bloodied line? I know:
it was just easier that way, it seemed.
Beware when you wake up from your
dream.

Another Dead Poet

Bill Scheffel, Naropa poet,
committed suicide July 8.
I knew Bill a little…too tender
for this world…too sweet…
took it all to heart too much.

Was it in protest of a dream he
took to be reality that made him
take his life? He was depressed,
we know.

Maybe it was because he couldn't
write the poem he needed to, so,
he used his life instead.

Burned up in a car, now there's
an image…
a poet, bursts into flame…
consequently, incidentally,
a coke machine releases a stick
of dynamite.

I can only conclude Bill was telling
us to wake up by blazing his body.
His ashes are the ink we use
to tell the truth.

Apotheosis #2

A moment
transfixed by a landscape
not focused on yourself.

A surprise birthday party.

You're fired
you're hired
someone gives you a million dollars.

You watch your child being born.
You are with your father when he dies.

You realize everything you know
is wrong.

Autumn Cannibalism (a painting by Dali)

Two human distortions meeting
in an embrace of consumption.
...fruition of Western precision/
machine/mind/melding with
human heart/spirit…
Houston, we obviously have a
problem…the soul does not
compute…
open the pod bay door…
Frankenstein's dilemma…
the soul is greater than the sum
of its body parts…

…to everything a season…
the season when the train
runs out of track…that day
when you go out for a pack
of cigarettes and never
come back.

Black Snake

black snake rising
generic evil
garden variety

behind the fence
over by the wagon
under the shingles

gotta go gotta go
let the whole world know

one thing and another
details bring me down
computer out the window

My baby left me,
but I could never tell
if she was ever even there.

goin' down goin' down
let the whole world know.

Burnt Masterpiece

"Take a masterpiece..burn it a little…
makes it even better." C. Trungpa

Burnt out on struggle, survival, ambition,
goals,
plans and dreams,
schemes for self improvement,
hope that things will get better,
so, now,
seeing perfection of things as they are.

"Chaos Is very Good News"

There is no
status quo
in chaos.

Don't bother
to look around;
no one can save you.

Sharpen awareness
and let go your ego:
the only thing
that can bring you down.

A samurai under a tree,
picking flowers,
the moment before combat.

Burning Man Mind

Burning Man mind…
Woodstock mind….
Monterey Pop mind…
Hip-hopcracy…
"Childhood's End":
Burning Man mind
takes over the world,
everyone freely themselves
working together
playing together
"power over others" outlawed…
not socialist or any doctrine:
no rules except the Golden one.

Burning Man mind:
artist mind…
yogic mind…
father mind…
mother mind…
ordinary mind…
first thought mind…
beginner's mind…
evermind…
takes over the world.

Clear Spot

"Everything's clear when you're cornered."
Trungpa

There is a point where words don't help,
where we must rely on perception…
call it being born.

Language is merely afterbirth
second thought
double take
square two
   useful only
      as afterthought
attempt to understand
what just happened
     that becomes
       history
(or her story)
   "Nothing to see here, folks,
move along."

Chimera

Hollywood vision packaged and sold
for consumption by the brainwashed …
Antifa blocking free speech in the
name of equality…
black is white, left is right, up is down.

NSA: No Such Animal…manufractured
reality…
hallowed hall of smoke and mirrors…
apology ball lickers…
deep state of denial…
anti human agenda…
mind meme nobots…
consumption of cognitive dissonance…
white male cliche massacre…
you've come a long way, baby.

Circe's Spell

Circe's spell
made pigs of men
seduced by the local Lethe
forgetting they ever were human
lost in the Matrix
of Manhattan,
of conflicting emotion
and primitive belief,
hiding behind heroin
of misplaced hope,
lost in the fun house,
funneled through reality tunnels
to the slaughterhouse.

Church Bells

Quiet evening sans fiestas and dogs
village center murmurs whispers
no wind or distant storms
bells ring a steady cadence
calm space echos of vastness
I wish this could be the last night.

Coming Off A Four Day Opioid Binge

My muse sits in the corner,
slouching on a chair
torn net stockings
smeared makeup
a broken cigarette
dangling from half opened lips
looking at me with an accusing smirk.

Clued In

Life is an open secret
understood by its clues
which are experiences
not concepts.

Even colleges, now, tho,
not very quick on the uptake,
acknowledge, give credit for,
life experience.

Intuition, that razor edge,
that connects the seen
with the unseen, is the
only book one needs
to learn how to read
the leaves on the trees
the pattern of a waterfall
why the birds migrate early
why I need to sell my house,
move to Montana,
take up knitting…
the unknowable,
the clean slate,
tabula rasa
on which experience is born.

Colors

I recently, within the last few years, have
turned old. I like to put it that way; "turned
old", because it reminds me of milk that's
turned or day old bread, a natural organic
process….nothing to be ashamed about.

I knew I was turning because getting drunk
was no longer fun. I didn't mind the bumps
and bruises that would appear in mornings
that I didn't remember where they came from.
While I was still drinking, I still thought I was
invincible. Only the increased awareness that
comes with sobriety led me to understand
that I was in the "old" ballpark. It was a new
chapter in my life: the "old" chapter, the last
one. Since I'm a young old person, I'm still
exploring the territory.

I'm sure getting old will get old after a while.
I'm still exploring the advantages: having a
good excuse for clumsiness, not remembering
names, speaking inappropriately, (although,
I always kinda did that) etcetera.

But, I'm determined to not go quietly. I wear
bright colors; rainbow socks for example,
beads and rings, partly so vehicles can see
me, partly for effect. I wear patchouli and
sandalwood since only dogs like the smell

of an old person because they are starting to
smell like food. Also, the colors are a warning
the way blue ringed octopi and tropical toads
warn other animals. Talk to me and I might
blow your mind, or, even make you laugh…
at least, piss you off.

Old Buddhists have a job to do. We must be
available, like breadsticks, in case someone
has a hankering to talk to one. You don't
always want to eat breadsticks, but they're
nice to have around. We Buddhists are always
open to serendipity and auspicious coincidence.
At least, that's what I'm saying now.

I'm writing a lot about old age now, as I wrote
a lot about love and passion, when I was young.
Obsession with anything is equally delusional,
but, being young, hormones were a good excuse.
And, other young people were equally obsessed,
so, there was an audience. Young people don't
want to hear about old age. Old people want to
deny and ignore it. So, F'em all, that's what I got,
and I'm going with it. Better, to my mind, than
just listening to elders list the present causes of
their near future demise. It's quite humorous to
me, actually, to watch bits of me fall off or fail, like
an old jalopy….Superman my ass.

"I am a verb", as Fuller said; a process, not a
"thing" that exists eternally, or, really, actually,
from a Buddhist perspective. Watch a time lapse
of a person from baby to oldster. We think we are

the same person throughout our lives, but, if we're honest with ourselves, we see we're not. If we haven't spent time in our lives to look into the phenomenon of existence, the default perspective is believing we exist, eternally somehow, particularly when our existence is threatened. In extremis, we call on God, or any of His names, to save us, like clinging to a rope as we're falling.

So, aside from the inconvenience, it's joyful to feel old and it's attendant accommodations after having sussed out life and realizing it's like going to a comedy club for a few laughs, and then, having to go home.

P.S.

"I grow old…I grow old…
I shall wear the bottoms of my trousers rolled.
Shall I part my hair behind? Do I dare to eat a peach?"

That's T.S. Eliot's lament about growing old and feeling like a failure. The fact that he wrote those lines means that he wasn't. But, Prufrock, the subject of the poem, shows what most of us are up against. "The unexamined life is not worth living." supposedly said by Socrates. Good point.

Celebrating Life

"I have lived.
Let us see if that is all." eecummings

Birthday party with drugs and ice cream…
different than when I was a kid,
except for the ice cream.

Not celebrating that I'm still alive, rather,
that I have lived, more than waiting for
something to happen
following the beaten path
not undone by circumstance
I took a chance
desperate for the truth.

Seventy one, I thought I'd be dead by now.
A lot of us hippies had that thought…a lot
died in that roiling of culture, jumping out
of windows on LSD, pioneers of spirit, naive,
fearless…stupid maybe, but knowing
something had to be done to wake humanity
from materialistic slumber; live free or die was
the choice we saw and acted.

"Like a fighter the soul must be constantly in
training lest it grow soft on an ephemeral
throne"   William Burroughs
Trungpa and Beethoven died when they were
fifty seven…Rimbaud stopped writing when

he was twenty. It doesn't matter how long you live. "Even Jesus wanted a little more time." The quick and the dead..."You don't have to be quick to live here, but, it's over."

What can I say about life? It's got a beat, you can dance to it...there's no alternative...be there or be square...ice cream....a red wheelbarrow...never arranged but always complete...a moveable feast...the party's just getting started.

We love to communicate, don't we? Look at all the languages...look at Billy Budd. My presence is my present to me and the world... why not? If no one reads me, did that tree really fall? That's why nothing ever happens until everything happens at once. Got me?

There's an old Buddhist joke: the Italian Godfather makes you an offer you can't refuse...the Polish Godfather makes you an offer you can't understand...the Tibetan Godfather makes you an offer you can't refuse or understand. This joke came about because Chogyam Trungpa was that very Tibetan Godfather...hence, the joke. The reason this is so, is because Trungpa's teachings went against our egos, rubbed them the wrong way. It was painfully true, so it was hard to listen to and harder to hear. It was an acquired taste. Are we clear on this?

Which was why Trungpa was hard to take for a lot of people. He told the truth whether anyone liked it or not….constantly, without a vacation. You weren't kidding yourself around him, and you knew it…it was excruciatingly delicious, steak tartar. Dare I say it? Spiritual vivisection….but…good! Psychic surgery without anesthetic… ruthless compassion. He was able to do this because of his training that had completely destroyed any trace of self aggrandizement in him. His presence was uncontrived and completely spontaneous…very intimidating to robots.

Our beings don't end with our skin. Our beings pervade space to a greater or lesser degree. This is easily demonstrated by our experience of some people walking into a room and lighting it up with charisma. Imagine if our minds were trained to be open!

Shifting gears…writing unfolds (unpacks?) like claymation…I love that I love to write… I'm constantly surprised what comes out of the old cabeza…I make myself laugh…I want to make others laugh as well…even philosophy makes you laugh when you "get it". Shakespeare's Fool is the model for all sage comedians. The gurus were known to be hilarious….but they didn't tell jokes.

I never thought my life would be this great…
that could be the drugs talking, but, still…
this is my birthday suite…enjoying my
temporary pleasure…don't mind if I do…
blah blah blah…there's room for that too…
boredom…has anyone ever written a boring
novel that was a best seller? There's no
Olympic sport that gives a gold medal for
standing quietly… American Indians or Zen
masters might be impressed…it's all
happening at the zoo….there's no
accounting for taste….mind if I cliche?

Burning Man or Gulag…those are the two
choices I see…Eden was always the goal…
get back Jojo…back to the garden…archaic
revival…that or the Morlocks take us
downstairs…live free or die…the character
of the conflict has never changed, although
many have transcended it altogether…the
tools are still available waiting to be used.

No need to end this rant because no
beginning…just a fun tip toe through the
Manichean wabi-sabi.

Culling The Absurd

Angry, infuriated, incensed, furious!
About what?
I forgot…could you remind me
by stating your point of view?
Oh, yes! Now I remember!
Those words you say!
I hate you…uh…them!
Because you use those words
you must be everything
I think you are…
everything
I think of people that use
those words!
In the beginning was the word…
it was all downhill from there.

Day Tripper #? (LSD rant)

La la la….dum dee dum….who cares?
Listening to: https://www.youtube.com/
watch?v=f2gyusjxBcY….live stream of
the Obama/Clinton takedown…la la la…
as the world turns…the states go
bankrupt…light-awareness-truth….less
of these means going into the dark age…
It ain't brain science, it's common sense…
"common sense is not common
knowledge"…it's going to take a lot more
than grease to stop the squeaking…what
a luxury…front seat in the arena watching
the gladiators of the Western World try
to take each other down…pay me now, or,
pay me later…Blake, Rimbaud, Kerouac…
derangement of the senses to pulverize
concrete mind…."the eccentric is the
basis of design." Wallace Stevens…(and
he sold insurance)…yes, the LSD is front
and center…no additives…birthday suit of
psychedelia…now what? …nothing to it
but to keep going…why psychedelics?
Isn't life confusing enough?…apparently
not…and, after all, who's keeping track?
Sure, we have to get from point A. To
point B., but most do that without thinking.
So, the real question is do we have control
of our own minds? What other question
could be so important? Taking things for

granted, which we all do, is the opposite
of being in control. And most people think
that if they're just going along, and there
don't seem to be many problems, that
everything is OK. Ignorance is bliss, from
that point of view. But, of course, it misses
the point.

I could sit, silent, like the stoned Mason I am,
but I can't seem to shut myself up, no matter
what people think they know. "To know is
to get lost" Nanao Sakaki. "Filthy Theatre"…
Joel Gersmann, exposing the Catholic
Church's pedophilia before it became
fashionable to do so. Fashionable to
expose pedophilia? Sounds strange,
doesn't it? Common sense would say…
but common sense is not common
knowledge, as we now know. If you don't
trust in your own intelligence, you're
screwed from the git-go, and might wind
up in Gitmo!! Stranger things have
happened, and will continue in the
out-of-balance world
we inhabit.

So, why? I don't know! So, I let it go.…
it seems to take care of itself naturally. As a
character of a play I was in said: "Make a
decision…just make it! Things will turn out
more or less the same anyway." (Sire de
Baudricourt in Anouille's "The Lark").

And so it goes, as Vonnegut was wont to
say. Holocaust? Armageddon? Paradise?
…and so it goes. They say Feb. 25 new
date for the end of the world. I wish they'd
make up their minds…on the other hand,
they only have to be right once.

The presence of the Lord. Shambhalians
call it "Authentic Presence". More than
charisma, or, more accurately, charisma
Is the outer manifestation of authentic
presence. Who had it? Gandhi, King,
Kennedys, Mohammed Ali…the truth
sticks out 'til it can no longer be
conveniently ignored. These people,
and Elvis and others, were constantly
giving us a clue as to how life could be
experienced completely, without hesitation,
with critical thinking and common sense
as the basis of joy: Be precise, see clearly,
know what is. In Buddhism, these are
called the three kinds of confidence.
That's why soldiers follow the best leaders.

Where were we? Ah, yes, as I was
about to say, who said that?

Day Off

MDMA while drugs are still not yet palliative,
not that I don't feel a little terminal. "I drink to
experience ecstasy of mind." said Kerouac.
Yes. I did too, and it worked for about fifty
years, then,I quit....not the ecstasy part,
obviously.

Day off? There was a billboard with the Dalai
Lama on it in India showing a photo of him
drinking a Coke@. The caption read: "The
Dalai Lama takes a break." Chogyam Trungpa
saw the billboard, and his response was:
"From what?"

Day Off. I retired when I was fifty three. Not so
much retired as stopped working.....plumbing...
my livelihood. It served me well for thirty years.
The minute I thought I could survive without it,
I quit.

I had a privileged upbringing, but I didn't chose
a privileged profession. They all seemed to be
traps; entertainment, law, writing all required a
certain amount of capitulation in order to attain
success. No one wanted to be a plumber...one
of the few remaining professions for outlaws. It
was perfect for me. Lazy? That's why I moved
to Mexico. Also, because the pressure from the
process of America waking up from it's

misplaced dream was becoming too intense…
the way it is now.

. . . .

Goodbye yellow brick road…you just numbly
don't get there…there's always a man behind
the curtain…the farther we get from the earth,
the further we get from ourselves…ashes to
ashes, after all is said and done.

When young, one thinks one is immortal…and
now, chronic ironic little reminders that life is
just a process, an ephemeral event. Just
because you have a name doesn't mean it's
not an illusion.

First "servietta", white butterfly looks like a
floating napkin. They appear at the beginning
and end of the rainy season here. It's too early
for them. They're probably confused along with
the rest of us. Progress was such a hopeful
concept…gave a sense of stability and purpose.
Now we're thrown back to survival.

That's why I'm ready to die…a little early,
maybe, but you never know. When young, I just
wanted to know what was going on…what was
life? No one even seemed interested. That's why,
when I stumbled upon Buddhism, I realized that
someone had figured it out. When I met my
teacher and realized here was someone that
knew and had worked it out, that's all I needed.

After decades of work, what I know and my
life are the same. No more struggle on the path.
So, unless I can help someone, be of some
assistance, I'm ready to move on.

It's hard to meet the Buddhist teachings. When
you do, there's no guarantee that one will connect
with them. Most people will agree that there's
a subtle, or, maybe not so subtle, nagging feeling
that something's missing…otherwise, there'd be
no religion.

I like Robert Anton Wilson's religion….where every-
body gets to be Pope, infallible unto themselves,
which, if you think about it, is the way it should be.
As the teachings say: "Even if the Buddhas of the
Three Times rise against you, you will remain in the
Indestructible vajra nature." I'll buy that for a dollar.

I had a course in college that was Zen meditation.
The instructor was a sensei from Kyoto University.
We would meditate for an hour, and then sensei
would tell a funny Zen story. A party was given in
his honor at the end of the trimester. Sensei got
quite drunk, and gave a teary monologue about
how he hoped he had done well, and that he
wanted to help everyone. It was embarrassing
for his mainly white, Protestant audience. What
we didn't realize was that sense was being
authentically Japanese in his drunken ramble,
that Japanese are allowed to be truthful when
they are drunk, which is why it's a nation of
alcoholic businessmen. When I was in Kyoto,

I saw a vending machine that had bottles of
Johnny Walker Red for sale. I didn't appreciate
sensei Nishimura 'til years later.

Sheeple….and the bleat goes on…don't say
we didn't warn you….this is what "2012"
was all about, the battle of good against
evil, "great awakening", "cosmic attractor",
"singularity", "armageddon" even. So, it's a
few years later. As Jack Kerouac said: "Walking
on water wasn't built in a day." (Died on his
toilet like Presley).

I write. Some people knit, ride horses…all
kinds of things. Some people like trains, I
like words. That's all It is. On the other hand,
art, communication, appreciation, transmission, evolution. I like
reading what I wrote, which
doesn't mean I think I'm any good at it. Practice
for next lifetime. One person in the world
thought I was good enough and published
me…that's good enough for me.

The end of my life is an attractor for me, not
in the sense that I want it to happen, though,
to be honest, sometimes I do…not out of
depression, more out of a sense of "let's get
on with it" or something.

Drunk Diamond

Nobody's perfect.

That should be the whole poem,
however,
some assembly may be required,
like,

don't pay attention to that gaping
hole over there…
or,

how many more years does a
glazed doughnut have?

That's the problem:
simple is simply better…
Occam's tape measure.

I drank so many years
sober's just as good...
the rest is coda

Drinking Absolute

"What'll it be?"

Kierkegaard was frozen for a second
in mid sit. He eased himself onto the
bar stool.

He had just come in for a quiet drink.
His mind was full of the latest theories
and calculations. The last thing he
expected was to be stunned by the most
profound philosophical question he had
ever heard.

"The usual?"

He had not yet even gotten his bearings
since the first question, and, here, a
profound corollary assailed him again into
stupefaction. He felt he was waking into
Einstein's dream.

Wordlessly, he got up and walked out of
the bar, the bartender, a quizzical expression
on his face, looked after him, wiping a glass.

Empty Heart

Garden perfect in wabi-sabi indifference.
When a soldier drops next to you,
you just keep walking.

What happens to the love when you die?
Where is the love when you don't feel it?

Civilization just another word for nothing
meant to last.

We have paintings, poems, music; captured
moments of beauty to be relived.

All that too will be gone.

The only joy is that beauty, humor, love arise
wherever the mind does.

Eternity of ephemeral circumstance,
serendipity of causality,
nothing left to chance,
wrote a song about it…
want to hear it?
Goes like this:

Empty Mirror

The Big Bang happened
when you walked through the front door,
when the boss told you to come to
the office,
when you saw your child being born,
when your teacher slapped you in the face.

Some things end, but nothing ever finishes
in the tamasha called samsara….
ripples of karma echo down the time wave.

We only know we were asleep
when we wake up from the dream.

Esoterrorist

Esoterrorist, aesthetic assassin,
intellectualaerealist, machosurrealist,
automagician, psycoconoclast,
third man, mythtery, open secret,
third mind, chiaroscuro bete noire,
manifest determinism likely story
gain the world and lose your soul
win the game and lose your marbles
surfing the crest of marvelous view
always danger of wipe out
never a dull moment just dull people
"Life is like getting on a boat
you know will sink." (Suzuki Roshi)
"'Why then, I'll fit you.'"
(Heronymo's mad againe.) (Thomas Kydd)

Elderberry Wine (for Elton John)

How can I ever
get it together
without a mind
that's mine?

The sea in the summer,
the sky in the fall,
walking out where we
could not stand

on a shore of sand
intoxicated to a man,
how can I ever
get it together
without my life in line?

There's a fly in the window
a dog in the yard,
"and the eyes of it's eyes
are as lost as you'll find".

"Drunk all the time
feel'n fine
on elderberry wine."

Fou D'Etat

They thought they had it all locked up.
With Hillary president, they take over
the world.
Elites drinking babies blood with the
rest of the people enslaved.
Oh, they thought they had it all
wrapped up.
"That's a wrap!" as the fans follow
Hollywood into the abyss.
They didn't count on common sense.
They didn't count on Trump and
military intelligence.
Halfway into their sixteen year plan,
Trump showed up, and they laughed.
He couldn't be a threat, they thought.
"We have sixteen ways to Sunday
to take him down." they said on live T.V.
Who's laughing now?
There's panic in D.C.…
their plan is failing…
they're starting to lose their minds,
and it's a thing of beauty.

Fresh Airspace Crossfire

Betray blame hangover
wild handler acid discussion
pounding creation senseless
jagged distorted believing
heat colliding bloodsport
perilous toy fairytale autopilot
stone grin cynical loveraping
barbaric conclusion explanation
hoaxer flake calibration disaster
it's all over now.

Fathead

Fathead

I'm a lazy bastard, I'll give myself that.
Even that statement proves
everything is poetry.

Fried astronaut stares out the window
on his ranch in Montana.
He thinks:
"I haven't seen everything,
but I've seen enough."

Luminous fundamentalist believer
batteries not included.

Human bulletin fanatic
always wound up too tight,
a clock with not enough time.

The DMT gnomes have learned
a new way to say "Hooray!"
You could meet them.

Art is magic is psychedelic experience
is unfiltered life is "Buenos Dias!" is
the start the finish
and everything in between.

Figures Of Speech

Letters of an alphabet
Colloquialisms
Public statesmen
Body languid language

Emotional evocative provocative inciting
words that bloviate communication
to the point of manifestation

Cliches that capture common captions
of a culture…

…which political correctness would erase
along with memory itself…
not on my watch

Gears Of Time

"Each spring the chrysanthemum's astringent
fragrance comes revealing the hidden mechanism
of machine within machine within machine."
                                    Wallace Stevens

Grew up in Midwestern thresher basic morality
meat and potatoes, corn on the cob, fireworks
on the Fourth of July…came out confused,
looking for something real.

No one expected the First World War, but once
it started, it didn't end 'til it was over. The basic
mechanism wasn't dismantled, so twenty years
later, it was back in gear and, once again, war
didn't end until it was finished. No one learned?
When you get on the wrong bus, every stop is
the wrong stop.

Ozymandias, The Bridge of San Luis Rey, 1984
all hint that we are enmeshed in a process that
has its Rube Goldberg aspects; many tears and
much flapdoodle signifying the tell of emptiness,
yet unavoidable, unless, somehow beyond time
and space, which is hard to find
in the marketplace….

…all supreme fiction of mind.
It's time to unwind.

Ghost In The Shell

Moving effortlessly, and then,
a glitch, an anomaly;
distracted by a stranger…
derailed by "Ah ha!"…
searching for the meaning
of a school massacre,
as if hearing a constant
echo: "Who said that?"
Haunted by our own traces
as we move through time…
aware that what moves
us is not mechanism or
machinery. Looking for God,
the itch we cannot scratch.
Vainly trying to give the
meat dream some legs
some permanence
some hope of forever.

Fresh Garbage

People are always looking for it…
literally and figuratively.
Somehow fresh air and sunshine
aren't enough.

This "poem" is hot garbage
going nowhere
sitting there on the screen/page
waiting to be stepped in.

An inconvenience, a distraction,
something to acknowledge
and move on,
                    hopefully,
an aroma doesn't follow…
some things we can never
get out of our minds.

We are attracted to garbage…
"Oh! Ravenous for Feces!" (Shantideva)
Fast food almost isn't fast enough!
And junk/snack foods to make sure
there's no gap in our digestive career!
We are attracted to garbage!
Michael Moore!
Of garbage and for garbage!
He's the poster boy for garbage media!
Garbage politics!
Looks like you got some on ya!

Everyday People

Square one
for everyone
all start
at beginner's mind…
makes no difference
what bag they're in.

It's just ordinary mind…
like your momma used to make
hot cookies…
Dad mowed the lawn.

Don't tread on me,
I won't be under foot.
Look me in the eye
or go bye bye.

Burning Man Mind
is all we need.
Love is all around.
Get over yourself, and realize
you're part of something bigger.
It's so much more fun.

A Poan, A Poem, And A Porm

No one says it
better than nothing.

I miss your shining face
nothing in its place.

I can't talk to you. I plead
the fifth of Jack Daniels.

Excerpt

"At the college interview I couldn't tell
them what I wanted to be, which may be
why I didn't get into Harvard…I hadn't
a clue…I just wanted to find out what
the fuck was going on with having a life
anyway…which no one I encountered
even seemed to consider…like life was
a freight train I was on, going where no
one knew, but I had to get with that
program, in some way, to be somehow
successful at something, while, all the
while, we were all barreling along towards
some unknown destination. It never made
sense to me…"

Published 2007. Written (?)

Hit Or Myth?

The truth just feels right,
which is what's meant by
common sense.
Even children know this;
nature is true to itself.

Cabal kebob kaboom!
Burning Man mind meld!
Breakaway civilization leaving
Homosap alone in the dust!
Nature is true to itself!

Chaos Cuisinard cyclotron
Cern certainly cajoles uncertainty
Perhaps portals? We don't find
The smallest particles because
There are none.

Besides some
useful tools, science is a religion,
a belief, ergo, just another way
of labeling the myth.

I wish I had a punchline for this,
but, at the moment, I'm stunned
at the stupidity of the apester.

.44

No chip on my shoulder,
I carry a forty four,
happy as can be.
Don't mess with me.
You can have your opinions,
you can have your belief;
debate with me and I'll
give you relief.
No time for Atifa,
no time for P.C.,
Donald Trump;
fill in the blank:
who is he?
I'm a Johnson,
any man's friend.
If you ain't square with me,
you might come to an end.
Love watching children play,
pretty women too.
You think you're one up on me,
I got a surprise for you.
Loaded and at peace
Is the way I roll.
The world is the Wild West now,
don't you know?
Armed and friendly is how I go.

Crank

Gladness grenades egg blank mushroom
dank and unapproachable just like mom
once it gets started it just goes by itself
automatic kick start seems to be the sun
got to deliver the papers mow the lawn
parachuting into bottomlessness now
we have sixty one flavors all lead to death
desperate to be with someone not a crowd
why won't someone pay
a thousand for this poem?

Apparent Emptiness

Nothing is solid, nothing lasts
except nothing.
Even the universe is temporary.
Apparently, most think there must be
something real…otherwise,
we wouldn't be worried about
change and death.

That nagging feeling, that hole inside
we cannot fill
mocking like Ozymandias
is, really, where it's at;
the source and the return.

Our minds are trained to think
so we can go to the moon,
whatever that helps.
Bravo!
The monkeys got off the planet!
Now what?

People can do so many things!
Why is it so hard for them to just be?
Many old people realize it's all a wash.
Why would they have anything to say?

Our lives are a swinging door between
our senses and internal space mind.

No wonder we get nervous…there's
nothing, no me, in between!

That nagging feeling that we missed
something…that there's something
we need to know, then, we'll understand.

Omniscience is merely having nowhere
else to go, that magic feeling!
"To know is to get lost." Nanao Sakaki.
The only thing unique about us is
we have to realize that ourselves.

Aimless Wandering

No agenda
no deadline
no intention
no path
no goal

no psycho babble
no confirmation
no obstruction
no projection
no destination

right here with the music
play it over and over
it's never the same.

Doldrum Day

Doldrum day clunky mind
tripping over useless thoughts
nothing to report even if there was
why even bother writing

section forty two?
art to patch a hole in the soul?
maybe the soul is just a hole
soul music a cry from the hole
full of emptiness
had enough of nothing
something doesn't do much either
maybe I'll get down on all fours
and try to make it as a dog.

Written From A Funeral

As if I was there watching
those still alive,
someone reading this,
Ouroboros,
what goes around
comes around,
more people than I thought
would be there.

I can say I'm watching
those still alive
as if I had already died,
what difference my words made,
the important dust that was my life
just a terminal
an outlet
station
coffin/box
back to the factory
guarantee expired.

Written Before A Hamburger

A mushroom/swiss/cheeseburger yum!
…a bit of Beethoven…watching planes
land in a desert on screen…friend's in
trouble…BUMMER…om mani padme
hum…bellyful of blunder…too young/he's
done/on the wrong bus in the first place.

Organic orgasm…how could it not be, and
why that just now? The carnivore in me,
waiting for meatgasm? Fill in the buns.

It does matter, which is why poem is snap-
shot of unique moment if only even of the
poet's mind, mentality meeting meat, any
random pop up of experience captured
on the spot, flash frozen the way mind
does with memories…a slice of the
hologram: enigmatic, sure, but it does
contain the whole.

What The Sun Said

Sun gave me that ol'
get up and grow…
with it's get up and glow
…no sun and we
wouldn't even bother.

Sun is committed for
billions of years…whattya
gonna do about it?

"I watch your civilizations
come and go…it's nice how
you try.

You write things down
and still forget…do the
same things expecting
different results.
How many times have
you invented the wheel?
It's an accident you
evolved at all.

I only keep you around
because of the comedians…
the universe needs the humor."

Goodbye Medellin Goodbye Escobar

The whole city is a brothel.
A white cloud yesterday to the right
of a double rainbow in the shape
of a "C". Cocaine capital pleasure
center first world industrial fun
built to lust and I crashed and
burned as collateral damage to my
friend's self destruction, the only
way the cocaine story ever ends.

This is what money can do penthouse
narco cheese palace with brass
bannisters and two hidden wall safes
should have been a clue the bad vibes
annealed to the tortoise shell mirror
his money turned to cheap pure blow
and he blew his little boy into oblivion.

Electric Hippo

Horrible ambiguous age,
jaw dropping coercion
of blackwater flamboyance…
oneupmanship is all the rage.

Pretend to send your child up
in a balloon…change sex, then,
change back again.
It's a sucker's market.

At My Desk

Post apocalyptic cataleptic
frozen by the age I am
the time I'm in
on a cusp of switcheroo
my desk looks like a battlefield.
I'm a casualty of a causality
I never saw coming, still invisible
to most people, but inevitable,
like when water recedes
before a tsunami catastrophe.

Might as well be sitting at a cafe
in Nagasaki that morning
when everything changed
without warning.

The day Kennedy was shot,
the world felt it.
Today, everyone going crazy
in anticipation of…who knows what…
but knows something just ain't right.
Anticipation of shoe fall;
size: infinity.

Vivid

Snapshot
sudden glimpse
adrenaline panic
mosh pit intensity
moment of
birth
death
orgasm
accident
surprise party
punchline.

www.ingramcontent.com/pod-product-compliance
Lightning Source LLC
LaVergne TN
LVHW040319200726
843493LV00014B/615